WALKING OFF THE ROOF

Anthony Clarvoe

BROADWAY PLAY PUBLISHING INC
56 E 81st St., NY NY 10028-0202
212 772-8334 fax: 212 772-8358
http://www.BroadwayPlayPubl.com

WALKING OFF THE ROOF
© Copyright 1999 by Anthony Clarvoe

First printing: June 1999
ISBN: 0-88145-162-2

Book design: Marie Donovan
Word processing: Microsoft Word for Windows
Typographic controls: Xerox Ventura Publisher 2.0 PE
Typeface: Palatino
Copy editing: Liam Brosnahan
Printed on recycled acid-free paper and bound in the U S A

ABOUT THE AUTHOR

Anthony Clarvoe's plays AMBITION FACING WEST
(which premiered at Trinity Repertory Company in
1997), GHOSTS (translated from Ibsen, Intiman Theatre,
1996), THE BROTHERS KARAMAZOV (based on the
Dostoevsky novel, Cincinnati Playhouse in the Park,
1995), THE LIVING (Denver Center Theatre, 1993),
LET'S PLAY TWO (South Coast Repertory, 1992),
SHOW AND TELL (Repertory Theatre of St. Louis,
1992), and PICK UP AX (San Francisco's Eureka
Theatre Company, 1990) are performed throughout
the United States. They have received drama critics'
awards in Boston, Chicago, Los Angeles, San Francisco,
and elsewhere. Mr Clarvoe has received fellowships
and grants from the John Simon Guggenheim,
W Alton Jones, McKnight, Jerome, and Berrilla Kerr
Foundations, the Fund for New American Plays,
and the National Endowment for the Arts. He was
born in San Francisco and lives in New York City
and the Midwest.

This is for Kate Heasley

WALKING OFF THE ROOF was written in 1997-98
during a residency at Signature Theater Company
in New York, which was generously supported
by the National Theater Artist Residency Program
administered by Theater Communications Group
and funded by the Pew Charitable Trusts.

The residency included a series of workshops directed
by the author. The following actors participated:
Debbon Ayer, Vivienne Benesch, Gretchen Cleevely,
Carl J Cofield, Beth Dixon, Tom Dunlop, Saidah Arrika
Ekulona, Jason Fisher, Debra Funkhouser, Matthew
Greer, Babo Harrison, Katherine Heasley, Neal Huff,
Noel Johansen, Sylva Kelegian, Jennifer Naimo, James
J O'Neil, Michael Ornstein, Matthew Rauch, Sean
Patrick Reilly, Christina Rouner, Willis Sparks, and
Susan Riley Stevens.

Thanks to Michele Travis for suggesting the title.

WALKING OFF THE ROOF was presented by South Coast Repertory (David Emmes, Producing Artistic Director, Martin Benson, Artistic Director) as a workshop production in their Pacific Playwrights Festival, 18 June 1998. The cast and creative contributors were:

KELLY . . . . Amy Brenneman
DANIEL . . . . Jesus Mendoza
LYDIA . . . . Katherine Heasley
BRETT . . . . J C MacKenzie

Director . . . . Bill Rauch
Set . . . . John Iacovelli
Lights . . . . Doc Ballard
Costumes . . . . .Nephelie Andonyadis
Sound . . . . Mitchell Greenhill
Stage manager . . . . Kristin Ahlgren
Dramaturgs . . . . John Glore, Jerry Patch

WALKING OFF THE ROOF premiered Off Broadway, produced by Signature Theater Company (James Houghton, Founding Artistic Director, Bruce E Whitacre, Managing Director, Elliot Fox, General Manager), at the Theater Row Theatre on 2 February 1999. The cast and creative contributors were:

KELLY .... Erin J O'Brien
DANIEL .... Chris Payne Gilbert
LYDIA .... Wendy Hoopes
BRETT .... Paul Michael Valley

Director .... Darrell Larson
Set .... Michael Brown
Lights .... Jan Kroeze
Costumes .... Jonathan Green
Original music .... Loren Toolajian
Sound .... Red Ramona
Stage manager .... Fran Rubenstein
Dramaturg .... Michele Travis

CHARACTERS & SETTING

KELLY, *a woman in her thirties*
DANIEL, *a man in his twenties*
LYDIA, *a woman in her twenties*
BRETT, *a man in his thirties*

ACT ONE: a bedroom, sparely indicated, as it represents two different ones.

ACT TWO: the bedroom and, gradually, the rooftop terrace just outside it. The last scene plays entirely in the open air.

The scenes are meant to flow seamlessly from one to the next, without blackouts.

New York City. The present.

ACT ONE

Scene One

(A bed. Off to the side, a rusty vintage car fender. Afternoon. Winter light.)

(KELLY and DANIEL are under a comforter. DANIEL is asleep. KELLY is awake. Beat)

(KELLY wraps the comforter around herself. She exits. Water runs. DANIEL stirs and shivers in his sleep.)

(KELLY runs back on, wearing a robe, carrying the comforter, which she drops near the bed. She inspects the top sheet, smells it, and mutters under her breath. DANIEL starts and opens his eyes.)

KELLY: I let you sleep.

DANIEL: We were running and running.

KELLY: Come on. *(She grabs her pillow and pulls off the case.)*

DANIEL: How long was I out?

KELLY: Couple of minutes. Come on. *(She grabs the pillow from under his head and pulls off the case.)*

DANIEL: Really? A couple of minutes? It went on and on.

(She tosses him his pants.)

KELLY: Tell me when we're dressed.

DANIEL: I'll forget by then. I've already forgotten.

KELLY: Sorry.

DANIEL: You were there.

KELLY: Hm.

DANIEL: Something was chasing us. We had a fight. With them? With each other. What about?

(KELLY *pulls the sheets from the bed.*)

DANIEL: Are you mad at me?

KELLY: Just need to put everything back.

DANIEL: We made love, I dozed off, dreamed we fought, I wake up, and you seem kind of brisk with me.

KELLY: I'm not mad. (*She runs off, carrying the linens.*)

DANIEL: I'm more tired than when I feel asleep.

(*He pulls on his pants. From off, a clang. A ratcheting sound. The low throbbing of a washing machine.*)

(KELLY *runs back in carrying fresh linens, a different color from the used ones.*)

KELLY: Any marks? (*She examines herself.*)

DANIEL: (*Checking her back*) No. No. Something here.

(*He touches the back of her neck. She scratches it with her fingernails.*)

KELLY: Now?

DANIEL: Just red.

(*She starts putting a fresh bottom sheet on the bed.*)

KELLY: I need to shower.

DANIEL: Can I join you?

KELLY: Your hair gets in the drain.

DANIEL: I won't wash my hair.

KELLY: Body hair. You shed.

DANIEL: Oh.

KELLY: Help me?

DANIEL: Sure. *(He helps her with the sheet.)*

KELLY: And last time after you'd left I found wet footprints on the rug. Men's size eleven. *(Tossing him a pillow and pillowcase)* Put that in that?

DANIEL: Sure. *(As he struggles to do so)* I wish we could just go to a hotel.

KELLY: *(Doing her own pillow, neatly)* Hotels are sordid.

(DANIEL tosses the pillow onto the bed. KELLY puts it right.)

DANIEL: It's like you have to make this picture. This sculpture. It's like this installation. Conceptual.

KELLY: How.

DANIEL: "The Happy Home". Every detail. One note out of place the whole thing falls apart.

(KELLY neatens the bed.)

DANIEL: Stop.

KELLY: What?

DANIEL: Stop.

(He kisses her. She kisses him back.)

KELLY: I'm so cold.

(He touches her. She responds. They fall onto the newly made bed. She pulls away.)

DANIEL: What?

KELLY: If anybody else were doing this, I'd say they were pretty evil.

DANIEL: Would you?

KELLY: Then I remember who it is.

DANIEL: It's you. You're not evil.

KELLY: No.

DANIEL: You have good reasons.

KELLY: I know.

DANIEL: You are perfectly justified.

KELLY: I know.

(KELLY *exits. Shower water runs.* DANIEL *pulls on a mechanic's uniform shirt.*)

DANIEL: Evil.

(DANIEL *remains as the lights change.*)

Scene Two

(*Same night, different bedroom. 10 P M.* LYDIA *enters, dressed for bed.*)

LYDIA: Why! Why why why?

DANIEL: It beats me, I swear to God, I don't know.

LYDIA: I have to get up in the morning, I'm covering Monica's breakfast shift.

DANIEL: Liddy.

LYDIA: I can't talk about this.

DANIEL: You've got to, we've got to say something.

LYDIA: I don't think I have to do anything.

DANIEL: I didn't set out to make you feel like this.

LYDIA: You must have known.

DANIEL: I didn't know it would be this bad.

LYDIA: If you had known, would it have stopped you from doing it?

DANIEL: Yes.

LYDIA: Don't lie to me.

DANIEL: I don't know.

LYDIA: It must have been really important.

DANIEL: It didn't mean anything.

LYDIA: It must have meant something. It better have meant something. Sex was ours, didn't you know that? This utterly private thing. I'd done things with you...

DANIEL: Me too.

LYDIA: Did you do things with her that we did?

DANIEL: We slept together.

LYDIA: Of course they did, don't lose your brain too. I know you did, that's not what I meant.

DANIEL: What did you mean?

LYDIA: Don't sound *patient*, okay?

DANIEL: I don't know what you mean, that's all.

LYDIA: Did you do things, with her, that you had not done, before me.

DANIEL: I don't know.

LYDIA: You don't—well, think!

DANIEL: No.

LYDIA: Why not?

DANIEL: We didn't get around to them, I mean, it was pretty standard early-days sex, introductory, you know, polite. Not ground-breaking. It was the basics.

LYDIA: Not so hot.

DANIEL: No.

LYDIA: Then why the fuck did you do it!

DANIEL: I didn't know before I did it that it would be like that.

LYDIA: What did you think?

DANIEL: That it would be better, I guess.

LYDIA: Than with me?

DANIEL: No!

LYDIA: What then?

DANIEL: Better than it turned out to be. Different.

LYDIA: Wasn't it?

DANIEL: Yes. The basics are different with somebody different.

LYDIA: Why did you want something different?

DANIEL: It beats me.

LYDIA: It's good with us, isn't it?

DANIEL: Of course it is, it's great. This... Before you, dating sex was fine, you know, it's sex, for God's sake. But with you, it's meant so much more, we've done things, tried things, felt so much, doing it, this...felt like I was exercising with somebody.

LYDIA: Why why why?

DANIEL: I'm trying—I don't—

LYDIA: You got scared, with me, it's too close, I'm too much, you're trying to blow it up?

DANIEL: I don't think—okay, something, something—

LYDIA: You, what, you, help me here I'm insane I need an explanation, you wanted to see, what, something, what?

DANIEL: It's been so great with you, I love being with you, we talk every day, together practically every night, we're sharing a skin.

LYDIA: You felt that.

DANIEL: Yes.

LYDIA: And you still.

(Beat)

DANIEL: Do you think I wanted to see how it would feel if I weren't with you? Maybe this was some kind of reality check.

LYDIA: I can't be with you right now.

DANIEL: Lydia.

LYDIA: You don't want to see this, nobody wants to see this. (She goes.)

DANIEL: Lydia. Lydia!

(She comes back.)

LYDIA: What!

DANIEL: I just didn't want you to go.

LYDIA: I can't look at myself, the mirror in there, I'm leaking from everywhere, everything liquid is leaving my body, I'm this dripping thing, my brains are coming out my nose. Hold me, you fucker, and tell me it's going to be okay!

DANIEL: It's going to be okay.

LYDIA: *You* don't know! God. I want to go to church again. I want to be ten years old, I want to wake up in my parents' house, I don't want this needy stupid body anymore, I want to be small and smart and loved and not need you. I wish I'd never met you.

DANIEL: Really?

LYDIA: God, yes.

DANIEL: Do you want me to go home?

LYDIA: It's too goddamn late for that now! I am sick in love with you. What am I going to do, what am I going to do, what am I going to do? Maybe *grief* is a kind of exercise. To make you tired, so you sleep. And time passes without you and the world goes forward with you not knowing, and maybe you wake up and it's a little easier.

DANIEL: Maybe.

LYDIA: You *wish*. When I was ten, and broke a bone, the first time, my foot—

DANIEL: Ow.

LYDIA: Oh, I wish you had just come in and broken my foot. While reaching for something else you wanted and forgetting I was in the world.

DANIEL: I never forgot.

LYDIA: I just wasn't reason enough to stop.

DANIEL: I didn't think it would be this important.

LYDIA: You might have *guessed*. You might have said, "I wonder if this might by any chance bother my girlfriend. On the off chance, what the hell, I'll pass on the quick generic fuck".

DANIEL: This is what I do not understand. I knew all that. I love you best in the world.

LYDIA: And you still.

DANIEL: Yeah.

LYDIA: I think. Maybe. Other people, then. Just don't matter all that much to you. Is, I think, the answer. I think a person who thinks like that just doesn't really grasp that the other people with whom he shares the planet are fully alive. That my pain counts as much as your pleasure.

DANIEL: I know it does.

LYDIA: No you don't. Just as much.

DANIEL: I know.

LYDIA: No you don't. I am as human as you. This is what you must not possibly know. If my pain were as real to you as the prospect of your physical enjoyment, you would never, ever have done this.

DANIEL: I don't know.

LYDIA: Not if you love me.

DANIEL: I do love you.

LYDIA: I don't think. You know, really. What that means.

(Beat)

DANIEL: Maybe you're right.

LYDIA: I'm right?

DANIEL: Yeah.

LYDIA: You don't love me.

DANIEL: I thought I did.

LYDIA: And now you think you don't.

DANIEL: Well, you're the expert and you have your doubts! I know that if I've ever loved anyone, I love you. I never felt like this about anyone. But maybe you're right.

LYDIA: About what? What?

DANIEL: Maybe what I thought was love was just a warmer kind of happier feeling than I'd had with anybody before, and I'd heard about love all my life, and I thought this was it.

LYDIA: You don't love me.

DANIEL: I think I do. But from what you tell me, now I
don't know. There was a video game, when I was a kid,
Tempest, you shoot alien space ships on the rim of the
galaxy, and I was very good, playing at expert level, up
to level fifteen sometimes, bonus lives and everything.
And then one day I have a really great game, and I get
to level seventeen, and they introduce whole new kinds
of difficulty and I realize, like you say, I have no idea.
I thought I was good at this. It turns out there are like
a hundred levels, I never found out how many, I could
never get up there.

LYDIA: A video game.

DANIEL: I am doing my best.

LYDIA: Christ. I should go listen to country western
music, this stuff happens all the time. Somebody's idiot
girlfriend. Do you know how long I waited for you?

DANIEL: No.

LYDIA: In that crappy plastic chair with a motorcycle
magazine in my lap and all the guys leaning in saying
you'd be back any time from doing that tow, while the
tow truck is parked in plain sight?

DANIEL: I didn't ask them to do that.

LYDIA: I sat there thinking, he's lied to *them*, he's out
hunting parts for his sculptures. What's his name,
I should know his name, it's printed on his shirt,
telling me I always smell so great. Like French fries.
You walk in and see me, and it's written all over you.

DANIEL: What do you want me to do?

LYDIA: I want you to be my sweet sweet boy again.
I want to be ten and have a crush on you and hang
around the arcade watching you play video games and
the other guys are mean to me but you never join in and

the girls all think you're a geek but I say I don't care
I think he's kind of cute with his fingers all over that
machine and when I break my foot I ask you to write
something on my cast and you do.

DANIEL: I'm sorry.

LYDIA: That's life. You drop your guard, you get
popped.

DANIEL: *Why*? I didn't ask you to do that. Why did you
do that?

LYDIA: Because when you truly fall in love with
someone, that is what you *do*. You spread yourself
open. That is what you want. You know this, you must.
I could not be this wrong about you. Is that what hurts?
Jesus, that I was just so wrong? If you're this emotional
moron, I fell in love with you, what the hell am I?
God, please, can't I just be hurt, can't I just be mad at
you. Don't, God, please, make this be me mad at me.

DANIEL: Be mad at me.

LYDIA: *Don't worry*. No, but when I broke my foot,
I didn't know, because I'd never had that kind of pain,
that it would heal. And I wouldn't. That my body
would get better, so I can't even remember which foot
it was I broke. But that ever after, I would know I was
breakable. How being broken felt. What will become of
me, what will I be now. This broken thing. This adult.

DANIEL: I love you. Best I know how.

LYDIA: Never see her again.

DANIEL: Check.

LYDIA: No calls no letters no communication of any
kind.

DANIEL: Got it.

LYDIA: What if she actually likes you? My God you're a shit.

DANIEL: What do you want from me?

LYDIA: Stay the night. Sleep out there. Okay, I've done it. I'm done. Sheets and blankets in the hall closet.

DANIEL: I know where things are.

LYDIA: Here's a pillow. When do you have to be up?

DANIEL: I'll wake up by then.

LYDIA: Good night.

(DANIEL *exits.* LYDIA *lies on her stomach and stares into space as the lights change.*)

Scene Three

(BRETT *prances in, mostly undressed, carrying a tray of Indian takeout. Same bedroom, another day. 4 P M.* BRETT *joins* LYDIA *on the bed. During the following, he licks mango chutney off the back of her knee.*)

LYDIA: I get the sense that your real life is someplace else.

BRETT: Is that okay?

LYDIA: Sure, I guess. So that's true?

BRETT: I don't like my real life. This is my fantasy life.

LYDIA: It still takes time, out of your life.

BRETT: Yes. I have to account for every minute, yes. But there's something fantastical about it too, because I think about it so often, my time with you, I remember it in such detail, like a dream, if you try to remember it takes so much longer in the telling, or a poem, a sonnet is what, fourteen lines? They can spend pages explaining it.

LYDIA: Is that why I feel like you aren't quite here?

BRETT: But I am, that's what I'm telling you.

LYDIA: I could never do all that remembering, all that storing up for later, and be here, just here.

BRETT: I seem what, abstracted?

LYDIA: Very aware.

BRETT: Aware is good, isn't it?

LYDIA: I guess. Self-aware?

BRETT: Not so good. You think?

LYDIA: Self-conscious.

BRETT: I'm very aware of you.

LYDIA: Yeah.

BRETT: And it seems to me you're the one stepping back and judging.

LYDIA: Never said I wasn't.

BRETT: Done. (*He sits up and wipes his mouth.*)

LYDIA: This is some very goofy shit you're doing.

BRETT: I love your body, what can I say.

LYDIA: You're finding a lot of uses for it.

(*He picks a container from the tray. He spoons noodles onto the small of her back.*)

LYDIA: What are you doing? What are you putting on me?

BRETT: Smell it. Feel it.

LYDIA: It's warm at least.

BRETT: Delicious.

LYDIA: This is fine and all, but I have to tell you it's not so sexy.

BRETT: No? I'm licking you all over, that isn't sexy?

LYDIA: You're having your lunch on me. It's arbitrary.

BRETT: How do you mean?

LYDIA: Plus I work with food. "Order up!"

BRETT: If you start to giggle, this'll get very messy.

LYDIA: Sorry.

BRETT: You want me to stop?

LYDIA: Finish your lunch.

BRETT: Almost done.

LYDIA: How would you like it if I covered your body in whatever you work with?

BRETT: Words, images. I'm in marketing.

LYDIA: Well?

BRETT: LaCoste shirt, Levi's jeans— (*Reading his underwear*) —Hanes. It's been done. You like working there?

LYDIA: Why?

BRETT: Just thinking.

LYDIA: About me?

BRETT: You could do better.

LYDIA: What, like what?

BRETT: I don't know.

LYDIA: Don't tease me.

BRETT: I'm not.

LYDIA: I hate a tease, you are such a tease.

BRETT: When I'm ready, I'll say.

LYDIA: What? Like where you work?

BRETT: Just thinking.

LYDIA: Because you're so happy there? Because all
the secretaries and assistants, I see them, lunch hour,
they look so happy.

BRETT: Didn't say you could be happy. Said you could
do better.

LYDIA: Not the same thing?

BRETT: As it turns out. You might like it, though.
Better than we do.

LYDIA: Why?

BRETT: It would be a move up for you.

LYDIA: Look at me in the shiny office?

BRETT: Kind of thing. There, finished. I'm not offering.

LYDIA: No. I'm not accepting. *(She stands and starts
getting dressed.)*

BRETT: Now why do you do that?

LYDIA: What?

BRETT: Cover up like that.

LYDIA: You're covered up.

BRETT: I'm cold.

LYDIA: Me too.

BRETT: That's not why. I'm also older than you. You're a
beautiful young woman. I love to see your body.

LYDIA: I am not a show. *(She exits during:)* I'm not going
to wander around here showing you my whole naked
body, that is not part of the deal here.

BRETT: There's a deal?

(She reenters, carrying his clothes.)

LYDIA: You stare enough as it is.

BRETT: I'm drinking you in.

LYDIA: Hm.

BRETT: I want to be able to think about you when we're apart. I have to soak up every detail.

LYDIA: I don't want to be drunk in or soaked up.

BRETT: What's wrong?

LYDIA: I think this is all an idea you're having. About a man's life.

BRETT: This bothers you.

LYDIA: Yeah.

BRETT: You've been bothered the whole time.

LYDIA: Yeah.

BRETT: Okay. There are times I go, "Look at me with the hot young thing." Is that bad?

LYDIA: "Thing" is not good.

BRETT: No.

LYDIA: I don't know why I'm being difficult. People do this. *(Beat)* What are you going to tell her today?

BRETT: About what?

LYDIA: The time.

BRETT: I don't know. Shopping.

LYDIA: Bought anything?

BRETT: Meeting then.

LYDIA: Who with?

BRETT: I can make them up.

LYDIA: Funny, you pretend I don't exist so you have to make up imaginary people who do. Don't you worry about all the ways the story might fall apart?

BRETT: I talk for a living.

LYDIA: How do feel about doing that at home?

BRETT: Are you worried about my marriage?

LYDIA: I'm interested.

BRETT: Why?

LYDIA: Why. If it's a good marriage, why are you here?

BRETT: It's not.

LYDIA: If it's bad, why are you there?

BRETT: It might get better. It's been a bad year or so.
It might turn around.

LYDIA: Is this the way to turn it around, you think?

BRETT: It might.

LYDIA: I kind of doubt it.

BRETT: I'm happy with you. Sometimes I'm even happy
at work. If I can be happy enough ways, it might sort of
spill over. Put less pressure on the home life.

LYDIA: What happens to you and me then? If the home
life turns around?

BRETT: You'll be long gone by then.

LYDIA: You think so?

BRETT: You'll patch it up with what's-his-name.

LYDIA: Who.

BRETT: Whoever you're doing this to. (*Beat. He starts
getting dressed.*)

LYDIA: So what are you going to tell her?

BRETT: Car trouble?

LYDIA: Come on.

BRETT: You got any ideas?

LYDIA: You went to church.

BRETT: What?

LYDIA: You went to church.

BRETT: What church?

LYDIA: I don't know, pick one. What faith were you raised in?

BRETT: Episcopalian.

LYDIA: Okay, you know where the nearest Episcopalian church is?

BRETT: Vaguely.

LYDIA: Go there, glance in, memorize a few details.

BRETT: Why would I go to church?

LYDIA: You were out shopping and you had a spiritual crisis.

BRETT: Why?

LYDIA: You need a reason?

BRETT: My life, a crisis in my life. Okay. I'm, what. I'm driving around. Driving home. When suddenly.

LYDIA: Gradually.

BRETT: I begin to feel.

LYDIA: Sad.

BRETT: Lost.

LYDIA: Troubled.

BRETT: More and more I've been feeling this lately. Does all the angst seem suspicious? Like I'm atoning for something?

LYDIA: Do Episcopalians atone?

BRETT: You're right, never mind.

LYDIA: Good question, though, not feeling guilty, just—

BRETT: Empty. Empty and alone.

LYDIA: Good, that puts some of the blame on her.

BRETT: She's not so bad.

LYDIA: Don't tell me that.

BRETT: Sorry, of course. So I needed to go someplace and think.

LYDIA: More than think.

BRETT: Pray? This doesn't sound like me.

LYDIA: That's why I like it, it's outlandish.

BRETT: And just then I saw this church.

LYDIA: Right, great. So you went in.

BRETT: So I went in and I sat there. And I stared at the sanctuary, and the air, you know that air in churches? The dust motes under the high ceiling, how the light from the windows beams through that high air and catches the floating dust, makes it look like solid things, like ghost rafters crossing. And I remembered how when I was little it felt like the roof had two sets of supports, the wood and plaster and the dust and light, so it would never fall on me. That in that room I was unconditionally loved, no matter what I had done, even if people kept talking about sin I never felt they were really talking to me, the whisky priests, the lay readers. And how angry I was when I stopped going, how betrayed, and what a fraud I felt sitting there now, but knowing I didn't have to feel that way, because something else was telling me that all I had to do was sit still and I would be okay. But it's hard to sit still and not notice what you're doing, and somebody comes and starts vacuuming the sanctuary, so I checked my watch and got up and drove home.

(Beat)

LYDIA: That'll work.

BRETT: Bye.

LYDIA: So call when you can.

BRETT: Yeah.

LYDIA: And I'll see you in a few days?

BRETT: Yeah. It's going to be a crazy week, so....

LYDIA: Oh. I'll wait to hear from you.

BRETT: Yeah. Thanks for lunch.

LYDIA: Come here.

BRETT: Hm.

(She holds him. They sway gently. She hums and moves in a slow dance. He yields to the motion.)

BRETT: What is that?

LYDIA: *(Singing quietly, with swing)*
Oh God
Our help
In a-
Ges past
Our hope
For years
To come
Our shel-
Ter from
The stor-
My blast
And our
Eter-
Nal home
Skee daddle waddle oddle

(They are doing a goofy dance together by now.)

BOTH: Bad duh Dah dah
Dah dah Bah duh
Bah dah Dah clouds away
Bah dah Duh dum
Buh dum Bee dum
Bah dee Dee dum someday

(They kiss.)

BRETT: Gotta go.

LYDIA: You can let yourself out.

(LYDIA exits. BRETT ties his tie as the lights change.)

Scene Four

(KELLY enters her bedroom, another day, 6 P M. She carries a basket of laundry, including the linens from the first scene. She sees BRETT.)

KELLY: Ah!

BRETT: Ah!

KELLY: Jesus, you startled me!

BRETT: I'm standing here!

KELLY: I didn't hear you come in.

BRETT: I'm standing here, can I stand here?

KELLY: Wo. Stand away.

BRETT: Sorry sorry sorry.

KELLY: I just got here, are we fighting?

BRETT: I—no, it's—I've about *had* this day, so just, don't...

KELLY: I haven't seen you since this morning, the day is not my fault, I am on your side. We're gonna start this conversation again. Hello.

BRETT: Hello.

KELLY: How was your day, honey? (*She puts the basket on the bed.*) Is this about work? Or the other thing?

BRETT: Not. The other thing. Please.

KELLY: Work, then, what, you didn't get the detergent account?

BRETT: I got the detergent account.

KELLY: You did! That's...horrible? You were thinking about her, huh.

BRETT: Nobody, okay, nobody, get off that, would you? I'm fine. Little shaky. I stand there wittily chattering, I'm on automatic pilot in these post-presentation Q-and-A's by now, I stand there like the crowd at the air show watching myself do loop-the-loops—wo! nifty!—and today I notice—hmmm—I don't know what is going to be the next thing out of my mouth. I always, you know this, fly by the seat of my pants, shoot from the hip, I wing it, I wing it for a living, brainstorming, KISH! KISH! Lightning bolts from the blue, around my head, from my mouth, I'm a what?

KELLY: Van de Graff thing, generator.

BRETT: That's it.

KELLY: Glass sphere, blue lightning.

BRETT: That's it, that's it, that's me, and the words, out they come, get this down, honey, and she does, and they work, you know, they're our livelihood, they're, they're, they're me, basically, as far as the working world is concerned, they're my foot in the door, my leg up, my handshake, my face that meets the faces that I meet, these words, I'm made of them essentially, and I had no control, today, over what was coming out. No idea, nary a clue, and now I realize, I don't know anymore who is the master.

KELLY: You or who?

BRETT: The words, the words, the words.

KELLY: I thought maybe it was about the other thing.

BRETT: Maybe it's that, too, I don't know. *(Staring down at the basket)* Huh. *(He rummages in the basket.)*

KELLY: What.

(He picks up two socks that match.)

KELLY: You don't have to do that. *(He folds the socks into a ball.)*

BRETT: I don't mind. *(He picks up a pillowcase.)*

KELLY: Really.

(He starts to fold the pillowcase. She takes it from him.)

KELLY: *Really.*

BRETT: What's the matter?

KELLY: Nothing. Look. You are a success, you jerk.

BRETT: Yeah.

KELLY: My shrink says there are some guys who can't stomach that. Success. Can't handle it.

BRETT: I can handle it.

KELLY: Always have, I've seen it. So what is this?

(BRETT shrugs. He picks up another pillowcase and folds it.)

KELLY: My shrink says that there are people think their lives are these big frauds, like fake fronts—

BRETT: Facades.

KELLY: —and they want somebody to call them on it, catch 'em out, so they do shit that'll get 'em busted, that'll bust up their life, so they can say to themselves, "See, I knew it all along, house of cards, whole thing."

BRETT: He thinks that's why I....

KELLY: Screwed around? Ding ding ding. The screwing around is you're pinching yourself, trying to wake up from this you know, fake dream.

BRETT: People only pinch themselves when they're awake.

KELLY: You're a clever guy. Always said so. My shrink says you have an insufficient sense of self.

BRETT: Your shrink says a lot.

KELLY: Yeah, he's great.

BRETT: I thought they just asked questions.

KELLY: How would you know?

BRETT: I can't stomach the whole thing, look, I talk all day, people pay me to talk, why should I pay some goatee-and-couch man to listen?

KELLY: I'd listen for free.

BRETT: Screw you, you're my shrink now?

KELLY: You're unhappy, you think I don't know? You think I think you wandered off, the other thing, out of some, what, sense of joy? I don't think you're that kind of guy, I don't think you were out there celebrating yourself.

BRETT: Why do you keep bringing it up?

KELLY: Correct me if I'm wrong.

BRETT: Why? Please. (*Beat*) You're not wrong.

(*Beat. She holds out one corner of a sheet.*)

KELLY: Here.

(*He takes it. They spread open the sheet between them and fold it, mirroring each other's movements.*)

BRETT: I'm glad I fessed up.

KELLY: Yeah.

BRETT: I got so sick of the constant sense I was convincing you of something.

KELLY: Our life. What it suppposedly was. *(Beat)* Is that how the other thing happened?

BRETT: What.

KELLY: You couldn't stop talking? Once you started? Couldn't help convincing her?

BRETT: Yeah. I think. Yeah. *(He takes the folded sheet and folds it twice more before he drops it on the bed.)*

KELLY: And us? Too?

BRETT: What.

KELLY: I do not want to think. That all we are. Is something that we talked each other into.

BRETT: It makes me want to not speak anymore.

KELLY: It makes me want to walk with my eyes shut.

BRETT: Makes me not want to go on.

KELLY: Wow. With work? Or... Yourself? Or...

BRETT: Or I don't know or us or something.

KELLY: Seriously?

BRETT: Kinda semi—yeah, sort of seriously.

KELLY: Well, we have to go on, obviously, I mean our whole—oh Christ your *face*! You really—

BRETT: We can. We can. I was just—

KELLY: Wait. Wait.

BRETT: I mean it.

KELLY: I didn't...I didn't know this. How could I not have known this? *Stupid.*

BRETT: Don't.

KELLY: *Stupid.*

BRETT: Honey, sweetie, don't—

KELLY: You don't want to go on.

BRETT: But we can, and—

KELLY: No. No.

BRETT: Look, you get a thought about things and
it spreads, that's all, you start to think what isn't
marketing, every object you own is supposed to
be part of your story—

KELLY: Listen. You don't want to go on. Isn't that
what you're telling me? Tell me what you're telling me.
Say it to me. Say it.

BRETT: But before you said—

KELLY: I didn't know, that's all, I didn't know.
You want to leave.

BRETT: No.

KELLY: Don't you?

BRETT: No.

KELLY: You don't?

(Beat)

BRETT: Don't you ever feel that there's a secret, and you
almost know it? Always, out of the corner of your eye,
you see the person who's all the things you aren't. You
can't ever meet her, you can't ever be her, you're stuck
with yourself. Don't you ever think, if I could have that
life, if I could live in that skin? Why do I have to live
and die just me? What am I missing? I mean, what's
missing from *me*? If I could just stand like I'm standing,
but somewhere else, for a while. So you go to that other
room, and it's strange, you don't feel at home, it's

exciting. But when we're in strange places, we, what is the word? Revert. We become our most basic selves. So there we are again. It can't be done, can't get there from here. Don't you ever feel that?

KELLY: So why go away from me? You'll still be with you.

BRETT: That is the scariest thing anyone's ever told me.

KELLY: What if I said. Yeah. It's like that. What if I said, I know what you mean. 'Cause that's just what it's like. For me. When I meet a man. And I want to fuck him. I agree with you. Good observation. Happy now?

BRETT: Not so much.

KELLY: No.

BRETT: So we're just here to argue. That's what we've got left.

KELLY: We are not everything. Nobody is. This just lets you put off finding that out. Which everybody has to do, if they're ever going to grow up.

BRETT: Maybe that's maturity to you. Maybe it's somebody afraid to grow *into* something.

KELLY: So the plan now is that you say horrible things 'til I throw you out?

BRETT: What will it take!

KELLY: What would stop this from happening!

BRETT: I can't stop it now, I can't just leave you flat, that isn't the kind of person I can let myself be, I can't stay and be who I want, and I can't leave given who I am. *Help me!* Tell me you don't want me like this, leave me, throw me out.

KELLY: I can't. I can't.

BRETT: Help me.

KELLY: It would be I'm saying I throw away my life, I won't. *(Beat)* This will kill me, this night, I'll never make it.

(She picks up a sheet. He takes a corner. They balloon the sheet open. They snap the sheet tight and fold it. He starts a fold she doesn't mirror.)

KELLY: That's not how I fold these.

BRETT: Thinking of Boy Scout camp. Flag duty. Let me see, like...

(They fold it his way, long. He folds it toward her flag-style, into a triangle.)

BRETT: Supposed to be this big honor, but you had to wake up before everybody else. *(He tucks the end of the sheet into the triangle and hands it to her.)*

KELLY: I wanted to tell you something.

BRETT: Hm.

KELLY: A thought I had. About laundry detergent.

BRETT: God.

KELLY: For a T V spot. About a woman.

BRETT: I don't want to talk about work right now.

KELLY: And why she'd want to get things really clean.

BRETT: Can it *wait*? I was contented! Can you let me be contented? *(Beat)* Sorry.

KELLY: Maybe what should happen. I think what we should do. One of us should go. For a while.

BRETT: You want to leave me?

KELLY: No. No. I think you should.

BRETT: Me. Go away.

KELLY: Just for a while. A little while. Work some of this out. Come back refreshed.

BRETT: How long? I'll miss you.

KELLY: Let's not put a date on it.

BRETT: A week?

KELLY: A little longer, give me a chance! Let me feel it!

BRETT: Two weeks?

KELLY: Or so. All right?

BRETT: And then I'll come back.

KELLY: Then we'll talk about what we do next. Timing. Logistics.

BRETT: This sounds like utter bullshit.

KELLY: You got a better idea?

BRETT: I could stay.

KELLY: You got a better idea that takes even a little bit into account anything I want?

BRETT: I guess not.

KELLY: Okay. Okay. That's that. Great. A little time, a little thinking. This'll be great. We'll get our heads together, figure out what matters to us most. Take a breather.

BRETT: You had something you wanted to tell me.

KELLY: About what?

BRETT: You tell me.

KELLY: Why? Do you have something to say? Do you have anything to say about anything I do? With anyone? Are you in any position to pass any judgment on me? We are just out there now. We are just. Anarchy. Ask me. Ask me anything.

BRETT: No.

KELLY: Ask me?

BRETT: No thank you.

KELLY: Don't you care?

BRETT: Don't need to ask. Got the picture. *(Beat)* Maybe it's empty out there, maybe the whole world isn't worth knowing one person inside out for years. Maybe we'll come back sadder, wiser, and we'll be so happy forever.

KELLY: What have we talked ourselves into.

(The lights fade.)

END OF ACT ONE

ACT TWO

Scene One

(Same bedroom, different day. KELLY *is where she was at the end of the previous scene.* DANIEL *is with her.)*

KELLY: Did you hear something?

*(*DANIEL *stands still.)*

KELLY: No...

DANIEL: When's he due back?

KELLY: *(Pulling off her shirt)* I don't know.

DANIEL: Six or so?

KELLY: I don't know. He's been away.

DANIEL: Will he call first?

KELLY: Sometimes the phone rings, I'll pick it up and say hello and hear a click. People leave him messages and I won't erase them off the machine, then I'll come home one evening and they're gone. Sometimes I'll be screening the calls, and someone will ring, and I'll hear his voice and I'll think it's him, but it's just the machine saying, "Leave us a message". Then I hear the machine rewind, that little scream, "eeeeeee..." Then all the old messages play back.

DANIEL: How long has he been gone?

KELLY: Weeks now. The old messages play to the end, then they rewind and delete.

DANIEL: Must be him.

KELLY: Or somebody who knows how to work our machine remotely. Though I don't know why they'd do that. *(Pulling off his shirt)* But I don't know the why about any of this really.

DANIEL: You could leave. This sounds awful. You could just leave. You don't need this.

KELLY: He's away. I can't leave him if he's away.

DANIEL: So he comes back, he finds you gone.

KELLY: I don't know. Funny to think of the place standing empty. Perfect little world. No people in it. Just the marriage. If I could afford the rent, I'd almost do it.

DANIEL: You don't have to stay here. You don't have to help pay rent on a place for both of you if you're the only one here.

KELLY: It's my home. Did you hear something?

DANIEL: No. What?

KELLY: Thought I heard a step in the hallway.

DANIEL: No.

KELLY: Shh... What haunts me is the thought that he *has* been back. Tiptoed up just now and listened at the door and heard me in here. Heard us. And instead of bursting in, left again.

DANIEL: Is there another way out of here?

KELLY: No. Jumping.

DANIEL: This is no good. The next time he calls, you pick up the phone.

KELLY: And say what? "I want you to come home?" He knows that. This whole thing is based on me wanting him to come home, he knows that.

DANIEL: Ask him why he's doing this. Confront him.

KELLY: If I spoke and he answered, that would be the end of you and me. If he came back, we couldn't happen.

DANIEL: You ever think what he gets up to?

KELLY: Every day. I've missed you. (*She kisses him, long.*)

DANIEL: I promised my girlfriend I wouldn't see you anymore.

KELLY: Oh. Then why are you here?

DANIEL: I had to. I don't know.

KELLY: This is what a girl likes to hear.

DANIEL: I think she's seeing some guy.

KELLY: She wants you to marry her.

DANIEL: I don't get it.

KELLY: She wants you to marry her.

DANIEL: It's a funny way of showing it.

KELLY: We've all, all of us in the vicinity of this conversation, got a funny way of showing it.
Why did you come back here?

DANIEL: I didn't think I would. Sometimes it's like my body just does things.

KELLY: Not you? Your body?

DANIEL: Me, but...

KELLY: Not. So you're not here. Just your body.

DANIEL: I'm here. I'm always back there somewhere, going, "You're got a fine woman, you don't have to do this". See, my body's always kind of been bigger than me. More popular. I mean, when we started talking, it wasn't a conversation, you know? Your body was talking to my body.

KELLY: So why are you here? Asking questions and dispensing advice, what, do you want to know me as a person before you kiss me off forever, is that it?

DANIEL: You said I was evil.

KELLY: I did?

DANIEL: Yeah.

KELLY: When was this?

DANIEL: Before, another time.

KELLY: I must have meant both of us. I can't have said just you.

DANIEL: I heard it about me.

KELLY: I'm sorry.

DANIEL: I've been thinking about that.

KELLY: You're meant to. That's why they made up a word for it.

DANIEL: For what.

KELLY: Things we do. So we'll think about them.

DANIEL: It's hard to put together. Me. Stuff I've done. Names for stuff I've done. Names like from the Bible. Names that stuff makes me. So it never makes a difference the next time.

KELLY: The next time what? Your body goes and does something? You get led around by your dick?

DANIEL: Hey. It's not like you have no idea what I'm talking about. Right? What do you get led around by?

KELLY: Point taken.

DANIEL: Jeez.

KELLY: Oh God.

DANIEL: What?

KELLY: You made me forget to listen. Nothing. No.

(*As he caresses her*)

KELLY: Are you religious at all?

DANIEL: No. You?

KELLY: I guess I'm sort of vaguely spiritual, but I was raised religious, so I know the difference, and I don't think vaguely spiritual counts. But who's counting.

DANIEL: Well. That's the question.

KELLY: He's counting. My husband.

DANIEL: What does he do, anyway?

KELLY: Well, this is funny and I think it's the basis of the whole thing, the situation, he's in marketing, he charts trends and responses and I don't know what all but he does focus groups, do you know what those are?

DANIEL: They get volunteers to talk about a product or something.

KELLY: While my husband and the clients watch from behind two-way glass. There was a day when I literally looked behind all the mirrors here, I literally did. Listen.

DANIEL: What.

KELLY: Jesus, the neighbors may drive me crazy yet. Just walking. Anyway, for a while I thought maybe he *was* a neighbor, that he'd moved next door and was watching me through the mirrors, that they were all windows really. I come up with all these bizarre scenarios to explain why the most important person in my life has up and vanished but I still feel him witnessing everything I do.

DANIEL: He is alive, right? Your husband? He didn't die.

KELLY: I think about that sometimes. Once I dreamed he was dead and when I woke up I didn't know where I was.

DANIEL: There are mirrors all over this place.

KELLY: His idea. I used to think it was mine, to make the place feel bigger, but now I think I remember it was his. He said I had no conscience.

DANIEL: You don't seem like that to me.

KELLY: Only him. We had a big talk about the marriage.

DANIEL: Did I come up?

KELLY: Nearly. But no, this was not about you. And we said some time away might be good. And that he would be the one who was away, because of how much of myself I've put into this place. And we didn't say how much time. And these were my ideas, I said them, which amazes me, because they are so exactly what he at his most nefarious might just plain *want* that it makes me wonder, have I *got* a self anymore? I keep looking around for it, cat without its kittens, gone, sweetie, sorry, sweetie, gone. We should have said how much time we would take. I think we didn't realize, I didn't, how much time there was, in a day. And I even know this because I cook. Take an egg, there's your day. Make a little batter, set it in the oven, whoosh, this huge soufflé. A thing can get so huge when there's nothing inside it. Cut into it for sustenance, it collapses on you, and that's my day.

DANIEL: You should get a job.

KELLY: I had a job. Which I quit to, it seems, not have a baby. Come here?

DANIEL: What.

KELLY: Come here? Send your body over?

DANIEL: I feel weird now.

KELLY: I'm sorry.

DANIEL: That's okay. I want to know what's going on with you.

KELLY: I can't believe I told you all that. Does it bother you?

DANIEL: Kind of.

KELLY: I'm sorry.

DANIEL: I wish I could afford a hotel.

KELLY: I've thought of that.

DANIEL: I know you think they're sordid, but—

KELLY: I would just think he's following me. At least here I know the mirrors are mirrors. Strange mirrors, you never know. In hotels they seal them to the walls. Come here.

DANIEL: Now you've got me thinking things.

KELLY: Sorry.

DANIEL: Do you think you might be doing this, with me, that you're doing something he might walk in on so it might make him walk in?

KELLY: How do you mean?

DANIEL: Like you could make him come back by being with me. Like you're trying to, I don't know, fuck him back. Like a, whatever, a buffalo dance or something.

KELLY: That's a weird thought.

DANIEL: Sorry.

KELLY: That's really weird.

DANIEL: I'm sorry.

KELLY: Not that I haven't thought it myself.

DANIEL: Look, I don't know why you're talking to me when everything I say, you've already thought!

KELLY: I know that.

DANIEL: He's gone! Why don't you leave!

KELLY: I know that I know that I know that I can do anything I want, right? Walk out, start over, pretend we never happened him and me, I could do whatever I felt like, I could be free and easy and wander the world like him, that's how I picture him when I don't imagine him cowering in some corner watching me get off with you, when I don't picture him helpless to know how to just come home, after so long, knowing every day away hurts me more, and so every day it's harder for him to face me, so he stays away another day, is how I see him when I don't picture him dancing with flight attendants, free, I could be free to do any damn thing but the one thing I want, which is to be here, home, with the man I love, just being here, everything here for me to see, touch, taste, and not just hear hear hearing all the time hit me I'm, hit me help me—

DANIEL: No—

KELLY: Help me stop me hit me—

DANIEL: No—what should I—

(She hits him. And again. He grabs her and holds her down.)

KELLY: Don't—

DANIEL: *You* don't—

KELLY: Let go let go don't trap me don't—

DANIEL: Okay! (He flings her away from him. Beat) Man.

KELLY: I'm a fucking loon.

DANIEL: Spare me, okay?

KELLY: I'm off my gourd.

DANIEL: You got carried away for a second. So did I.

KELLY: I don't know what you see in me.

DANIEL: Man.

KELLY: What do you see in me? What do you think you're doing, being here?

DANIEL: You had something going on inside you. I wanted to know.

KELLY: Now you've seen it.

DANIEL: I guess so.

KELLY: You should go. He might come.

(She exits. DANIEL *stays where he is, the lights change, and the bed moves away.)*

Scene Two

(Another day. On a terrace just off a bedroom. 6 P M. DANIEL *polishes the vintage car fender, now perfectly finished.* LYDIA *enters through the bedroom, in interview clothes.)*

LYDIA: Ask me how it went!

DANIEL: How'd it go?

LYDIA: I don't know, but—

DANIEL: Bet you did fine.

LYDIA: I think I did great.

DANIEL: I bet you did.

LYDIA: I didn't make that guy look bad, recommending me, which was what I was mainly worried about, given I don't really know do I even want the job. But it felt good, you know, to get in there and hold my own. He

presented me to them, I realized, yeah. I'm presentable.
I could do this.

DANIEL: Look at you.

LYDIA: What.

DANIEL: You look so normal.

LYDIA: Boring, yeah, I know.

DANIEL: No, what? Adult.

LYDIA: Somebody said I had real presence.

DANIEL: You do.

LYDIA: *(Looking at her suit)* I don't think they could tell
I got this secondhand. *(Seeing his work)* Look at this.
It's beautiful. Is it for a sculpture?

DANIEL: It's a fender.

LYDIA: Yeah.

DANIEL: It's for a car.

LYDIA: It must have taken a lot of time.

DANIEL: I've been working on it down at the shop.

LYDIA: I'd never have the patience.

DANIEL: It's got this really deep surface now.

LYDIA: Like it's the same at the core as on the surface.
Nothing hidden. Clear, clear through.

DANIEL: It's like...I don't know. Something.

LYDIA: Lake water. Evening. No breeze.

DANIEL: I found it months ago, parts hunting,
and I thought, cool.

LYDIA: To use for a construction.

DANIEL: But I kept looking at it, I said, sure, use it to make something new. Or. Make *it* new. It's already something. In itself. I guess it's not so good for much.

LYDIA: Why not?

DANIEL: Well, *I* think it would be. It would be the high point of any car. Someone could take this and in place of a dinged-up, banged-up fender they could put this.

LYDIA: They could.

DANIEL: Or it could be a sign, like those old, on shops, hanging over the street, in history. A shoemaker would have a great big shoe? This could hang in front of where we are, and people would know. Don't you think?

LYDIA: Yeah.

(She kisses him. He reaches for her.)

LYDIA: Mm, careful, your hands—

DANIEL: I washed them just now, I haven't been—

LYDIA: I'll change out of this, and.... *(She takes his hands and looks at them.)* This is what they look like when they're clean now? *(She touches his hands with her fingers.)*

DANIEL: What's my fortune?

LYDIA: All these scuffs and cuts and dings. So rugged. *(Giving little kisses to his hands)* Mm.

DANIEL: What? Oh. *(He reaches for her.)*

LYDIA: Careful careful.

DANIEL: Here. *(He touches her under her suit.)*

LYDIA: Mm. *(Touching him)* Huh.

DANIEL: What.

LYDIA: Oh, if I, if this was how I dressed all the time, if I were some big executive woman, I bet this would be my fantasy.

DANIEL: Tell your fantasy.

LYDIA: It isn't mine, though it's...mm...it's the fantasy of the person I wish I could be. Mm.

DANIEL: Tell me.

LYDIA: I'd needed some work on my Beemer.

DANIEL: Body work.

LYDIA: Hm mm. And I come into your garage to pick it up.

DANIEL: In your perfect suit.

LYDIA: And you'd be rubbing the fenders on my car. So shiny.

DANIEL: So slick. The chamois slides right off them.

LYDIA: Like they were wet. Oh mm. I'd watch you from behind.

DANIEL: I'd see you watching me from behind, I'd see your reflection in the finish.

LYDIA: "Isn't my car ready yet?"

DANIEL: So you're this rich ball buster, huh?

LYDIA: You just keep stroking. You'd say—

DANIEL: "Almost ready, just need to rub this out".

LYDIA: God. "Well, my powerful executive husband and I need it tonight if we're going to make it out to our place at the lake".

DANIEL: So you're married in this.

LYDIA: Not me, I'm telling you, this, like, fantasy me, the business woman with the husband the executive. And you'd be this hot young thing who's good with his hands. All sweaty. Mmmm yeah. You want to go inside or stay here? *(Beat)* What's wrong?

DANIEL: I didn't want to be... I don't want that again.

LYDIA: But... Oh.

DANIEL: I just want to be us. Okay?

(Beat)

LYDIA: This neighborhood never did take off.

DANIEL: Not yet.

LYDIA: How many years are there in a "yet"? Back home when I dreamed of it here, I thought, if only I could get here, then, boy, then.... This was supposed to be a jumping-off place. Not our real life. I'm gonna get changed and start dinner. *(She turns to go.)*

DANIEL: Liddie? Do you want to get married? I think we should. I mean I want to. I mean I think it would be a good thing. Not like just a happy thing, I mean a happy thing too but. A good thing. I would be better. I would be a husband. We wouldn't be just hanging, you know? We'd say, this is what we are. So we wouldn't make the same kind of mistakes. We'd know what we were doing. I would be good. You're not saying anything.

LYDIA: Too much has happened. Danny.

(Beat)

DANIEL: I've got this whole place just about pictured in my imagination.

LYDIA: I bet it's lovely.

DANIEL: It is, it is. I see us happy here.

LYDIA: I know. I know, love.

(He stares at his fender.)

DANIEL: It is a sculpture.

LYDIA: Told you. It's beautiful.

DANIEL: I know what it needs. *(Standing)* Have you got your keys?

LYDIA: Sure, what do you need to go get?

(She hands him the keys. He puts a long scratch down the length of the fender.)

LYDIA: Danny!

(He adds couple of short slashes. He steps back and looks at it.)

DANIEL: Now it's right.

(The lights change. DANIEL picks up his fender and exits. LYDIA stares into space.)

Scene Three

(BRETT joins LYDIA. Another evening, another terrace. 10 P M.)

LYDIA: You're not even wearing a watch.

BRETT: No.

LYDIA: Me neither.

BRETT: No.

LYDIA: Because it doesn't matter what time it is, there's no story to tell, we're just....

BRETT: Here.

LYDIA: I still can't believe it.

BRETT: Believe it.

(They kiss.)

LYDIA: Okay, I believe it. What do you want for breakfast? I want to make you a big fancy breakfast. You like waffles? I brought the waffle iron, I haven't used it for years, in the morning I can wake up before you and cook you food.

BRETT: That sounds great.

LYDIA: Good. That's what I'll do.

BRETT: You make it sound like you never made anyone breakfast before.

LYDIA: He didn't eat breakfast. Coffee and out.

BRETT: Low-maintenance guy.

LYDIA: I guess, for an artist.

BRETT: I thought he was a mechanic.

LYDIA: It turned out he was. You, you're an artist.

BRETT: Sure.

LYDIA: Oh, sweetie, listening to you? You're an artist, you are.

BRETT: I'm a bullshit artist.

LYDIA: Hey. And look at you, so beautiful.

BRETT: Beautiful?

LYDIA: Don't tell me you don't know.

BRETT: I don't.

LYDIA: Oh, the way the women want you?

BRETT: They do?

LYDIA: Come on. You see them look at you.

BRETT: Sometimes. I guess.

LYDIA: Sometimes he guesses, listen to him. I mean, come on, I wasn't your only affair, I know.

BRETT: What?

LYDIA: I wasn't, was I? Your only affair.

BRETT: Define affair.

LYDIA: I thought so.

BRETT: You were my only serious affair.

LYDIA: Define serious.

BRETT: The only one I felt I had to confess about.

LYDIA: It must have been awful for her, finding out.

BRETT: I'd thought it would come as a terrible shock.
I hadn't thought she was the sort of person who'd do
something like that.

LYDIA: What sort of person is that?

BRETT: The sort of person who...

LYDIA: Would have an affair.

BRETT: Yeah.

LYDIA: Like with a married man or something.
A slutty sort of person like that.

BRETT: No. You are not that sort of person either.
You haven't made a habit of this sort of thing,
have you?

LYDIA: Of course not.

BRETT: See?

LYDIA: I wouldn't have thought I'd be the sort of
person who would do that kind of thing at all.

BRETT: Well. I'm glad you did.

LYDIA: Me too.

(He kisses her.)

LYDIA: So was there anybody after me?

BRETT: How do you mean?

LYDIA: While we were on hiatus.

BRETT: When I fessed up and you and what's his name were....

LYDIA: Yeah.

BRETT: No.

LYDIA: No?

BRETT: No.

LYDIA: Do you mean not at all or just not a serious one?

BRETT: Hey. Enough.

LYDIA: Why were you so sure that she'd never?

BRETT: I thought she was different from people like you and me.

LYDIA: Like how?

BRETT: She always seemed to have this very vivid conscience.

LYDIA: Why did you leave?

BRETT: I've told you this.

LYDIA: And now that you're here you're writing her valentines.

BRETT: What, are you jealous of her? I left her and now I'm with you.

LYDIA: Yes. You loved her. And you left her and now you're with me. I'll never be able to let you out of my sight, will I.

BRETT: Meaning what?

LYDIA: Meaning as long as we're talking about sorts of people, you are the sort of people who seem to kind of need to screw around.

(Beat)

BRETT: Oh God. I did not go through this. I did not
go through all this. To be with a different woman
having the same fucking fight. I changed my life!
I have changed my life!

LYDIA: Good, great, okay, sweetie, that's wonderful,
I know, I know what you've gone through—

BRETT: You have no idea.

LYDIA: No. You're right. I was just asking one thing,
that's all, as a gauge, as a way, for myself, to judge, no,
to see, if you were happy, if we could ever... Have you
thought, that's all, since us, of maybe ever wanting to....

BRETT: Screw around. Why are you asking me this?

LYDIA: I want to know you! The man I loved and
thought I knew, he broke my heart and I still loved him
for so long after, this stranger, but I, with you, which I
never would have thought, I want to know somebody.
Before I give my heart to you, which I can do, even
now, after everything, I can still, but before I do,
I have to, yes, I have to know. Is it all gonna happen
to me again?

BRETT: I'm somebody different. It's different with
somebody different.

LYDIA: I have heard that sentence before. I have heard
him say that exact sentence.

BRETT: What he did is not my fault!

LYDIA: No. But maybe it's always like you said.
Different guy, same fight. Please, just, and I'll believe
you, I want to believe you. Do you think. You might
ever feel you had to screw around on me?

BRETT: No. I don't... "Around". I don't... Look. That has
been part and parcel of a lot of other things, this need to
have anything to feel good about, this childish need to

look outside myself for some kind of happiness,
some sense of worth—

LYDIA: Can I say—

BRETT: It would be great if I could finish the sentence—

LYDIA: Okay, okay. Finish.

BRETT: I'm just trying to connect the thoughts—

LYDIA: Finish your sentence. This need for a sense of
worth.

BRETT: A kind of pride, admittedly false, or confidence,
obviously misplaced, that some sort of tawdry skulking
sexual misbehavior is nothing but a weak stab at, a
substitute for, so I think I should just get used to the
fact that those things are pointless to look for in my lie,
my life I mean, that those things won't be happening
until I learn to "like myself", you know, as myself,
but a different self than the centerless kind of unhappy
basically self that I am now and that hurt you all so
unforgivably, so I think I should become pretty much
a very different person, since that's what I would have
to do to actually know that I could promise that I
would never again do any screwing around, okay,
I'll just be on my way until I'm somebody you all
feel you can actually accept for who he is, which
understandably you can't now, given the potential
for harm that I embody, just by the way I make these
uncompassed moral choices in my behavior, because
really as I think about it what happened was that I
had so given over all sense of myself to all of you,
the reality, you know, of me, I literally felt so bound
to your standards for my behavior and so for my self,
standards which are so so so much higher than mine,
you see, all these mistakes in behavior, habitual
mistakes, so habitual that they weren't isolated
accidents, random events, but actually my personality,
these mistakes you all find yourselves so constantly

endlessly having to correct, well, in the face of this
ceaseless effort to help me maintain these hitherto
unimagined-by-me standards, I just kind of gave
up you know any sense of self-knowledge or self-
governance, in the way that, say, people under a regime
of some kind all go raping and looting because they've
had such tight societal controls they've lost all knack
for controlling themselves, and so with me I think
I'd literally gotten to the point that in response to this
omniscient scrutiny I literally felt that if you couldn't
see it, I must not be doing it, that it must be someone
else, and not me.

LYDIA: Finished?

BRETT: Nearly. All of which was wrong, so wrong,
to make you all my conscience, to let that happen,
mistake, bad mistake to have developed this kind of
not-self walking around waiting for some authority
figure namely you to come and punish my
transgressions, to count on that and thus to feel, what,
justified, no, in evading it, as if there were some may
the best man win sort of battle for my soul where the
only behaviors left to me, that were my own, and not
subject to your standards, were bad, covert, catch me if
you can, cops and robbers, Spanish Civil War sabotage,
you rumble over the bridge I blow it up and if you
catch me I'm shot at dawn sort of life, well, and isn't
that a recipe for disaster, these are relationships I
entered into freely for God's sake not some war of
occupation, I volunteered for this, fell in love, knew
all the consequences, of course no one can know the
day-to-day consequences, the life that results when
you fall in love with someone, you think you know,
you think you'll have some sense of the life you'll have,
the person it'll make you, how much of your self you'll
have left, but all you can do is try, under the constant
tutelage of the one you love, the unending tutelage,

thinking maybe someday I'll achieve the self I'm so
clearly falling short of, and then, well, then I'll be
accepted for what I am, and loved, you know, for that,
because I will deserve to be, as I clearly don't now, I'm
loved, now, undeservedly, loved, taking love, on credit,
paying back only interest, never principal, never
principles, clearly deficient in principles, but loved,
with this love that's like a line of credit, this forgiveness
of debts, where I take so much more than I can ever
give back unless I just declare myself bankrupt,
surrender and go into exile, find some little offshore
island I can live on and demonstrate my ability to
govern myself while I long for a return to my home,
anyway, that's the story, all my fault.

LYDIA: Okay—

BRETT: So so so so sorry.

(*She kisses him.*)

LYDIA: Enjoy yourself.

(LYDIA *exits.* BRETT *stares into space. The lights change.*)

Scene Four

(KELLY, *carrying coffee cups, joins* BRETT. *Another day,
another terrace. 2 P M.*)

BRETT: I hardly know anybody dead. Is that true?
My father. Grandparents, sure. But my age. No. No?

KELLY: Here's coffee. You're welcome.

BRETT: Are we speaking?

KELLY: You are, certainly.

BRETT: To each other? Maybe I'm just musing aloud.

KELLY: Muse away.

BRETT: Play with me. I have a right.

KELLY: We are dividing things up. That is why you are here.

BRETT: Yes.

KELLY: We talked about this.

BRETT: Yes.

KELLY: We're dividing things up.

BRETT: I know.

KELLY: That's all.

BRETT: That is very much all.

(Beat)

KELLY: Ken Honeychurch. Is your age and dead.

BRETT: Mm.

KELLY: David Garfinkle.

BRETT: Ernie Kerns. But all of them—I didn't know them well, just worked with them or whatever, then years later I hear they died years before. From someone closer to them. I'm saying I've never commenced an acquaintance, developed it over years, then had it abruptly interrupted or slowly forced into closure by death. It's the age.

KELLY: That you are?

BRETT: That we're in. No wars. No epidemics.

KELLY: There have been wars, you haven't fought in them. Of course there have been epidemics.

BRETT: Which have left my loved ones untouched. I have strolled through history unscathed.

KELLY: And you're complaining.

BRETT: No, it's wonderful. Just a mite thin.

KELLY: What prompted this line of thought? *(Beat)* I'm close to you.

BRETT: Yes.

KELLY: And not dead.

BRETT: No.

KELLY: Is that the problem?

BRETT: I was musing over what my life would be like without you in it, and as my mind was going over the various ways that that could possibly be, yes, the thought arose.

KELLY: So if I were to, oh, walk off this terrace right now. Just take ten steps from this spot.

BRETT: You couldn't.

KELLY: Sure I could.

BRETT: Eight at the most.

KELLY: They would get smaller as I got closer to the edge.

BRETT: You've thought about this.

KELLY: I'm thinking of diving boards and working by extension.

BRETT: It's not the same.

KELLY: Who knows? In that state of mind, maybe I could walk like I did when I knew that a cannonball would hurt, but I would make a big splash on my family.

BRETT: It is not the same as a diving board. There's no bounce. It's a diving *platform*. And when you make a cannonball, *you* do not make a splash, the water does. Whereas if you walked off of there, you would do the splashing.

KELLY: So if I did jump, you were thinking, you would finally know someone dead.

BRETT: Absolutely not. Suicide? No, you committing suicide would be incomprehensible to me, it would throw my every memory and impression of you into an utterly new light, I'd feel I'd never known you. Like infidelity.

KELLY: You're saying we never knew each other.

BRETT: So it seems. Look, if somebody makes a dozen suicide attempts, she's suicidal. If she tries it once and succeeds, ditto. Same with adultery. You're adulterous. You are or you aren't. You are.

KELLY: So are you!

BRETT: Well, I knew it about me! I didn't want to be that man anymore. So I came clean. I wanted to be worthy of who I thought you were. There I was, crawling, and all the time you were right down there with me.

KELLY: It wasn't me, somehow.

BRETT: Who was having the orgasms, that was you, yes?

KELLY: This is very painful.

BRETT: Who's having the pain?

KELLY: Me, me.

BRETT: To both questions.

KELLY: I didn't know I could. So I didn't know how to stop.

BRETT: You said you could walk off this terrace.

KELLY: So I won't. I know how to stop myself. I've lived with that temptation for a long time, teenage time. The freedom of it.

BRETT: The Emergency Exit.

KELLY: But I didn't know that about pleasure. Me pleased. *(Beat)* If you had thought I was capable of it, this very human thing, you wouldn't have married me?

BRETT: N O spells no.

KELLY: I could walk off this roof then and it would be no loss.

BRETT: Not of anyone I know especially well.

KELLY: And you could be a widower. In weeds. Widower's weeds.

BRETT: Catchy. Up to you. *(Beat)* Thing is. If I had known. That *I* were capable of it. I wouldn't have gotten married either. This is not who I wanted to turn out to be.

KELLY: Lots of people have had this kind of trouble.

BRETT: If everyone were jumping off the Brooklyn Bridge, would you do that, too?

KELLY: Sure I would. Look at people in warfare, people in epidemics. Old couples, one goes, the other drops two weeks later, everybody goes "aw". They had a love that worked in concert with the forces of nature, they can somehow command death to do love's bidding, not completely, not to beat him back, but in compromise, because all love's a compromise with death, they can say, "Take him and you have to take me too". And death, though not defeated, nods in acquiescence and extends his other hand.

BRETT: I won't have that.

KELLY: You still could.

BRETT: I could. But I won't.

KELLY: Some people just go into counseling.

BRETT: Jason and Medea did not get counseling.
The Greeks did not all sit down and talk it out together,
they slew each other with weapons that had names.

KELLY: Resulting in what?

BRETT: Western Civilization. You've been counseled
and look at you, it did not make you well.

KELLY: It helped make me better.

BRETT: It didn't make you good. It made you think your
needs were of unnatural importance.

KELLY: I have never. In any of this. Put any blame
on anyone but me. Have I. Never said "driven to it".
Never said, "pushed away". Never said "need".

BRETT: Whose? Not yours, surely, you didn't do it.

KELLY: Of course I did, sweetie. I know I did.

BRETT: And now you *have* said those words, "driven",
"pushed". I'm not an idiot, I know when weapons are
brandished, even if they don't go off. Why stop there?
"Cuckolded"! "Inadequate"! "Cold"! "Well no wonder,
I mean, have you ever listened to the man, wouldn't it
make you just want to go out and fuck!"

(Beat)

KELLY: Who's inadequate? You or me?

BRETT: I was quoting. Our friends, in the future, or now
and long past, depending on how widely this is already
known.

KELLY: It's not. It isn't.

BRETT: Liar. You don't know.

KELLY: It isn't, he...

BRETT: Finer than that, is he? Oh good. Good for you.

(Beat)

KELLY: You're not inadequate. That's not why.

BRETT: Good, thanks. But you don't *know* why.
So it could be anything.

KELLY: I know it couldn't be that you're inadequate like
I know I wouldn't walk off this roof. That certain.

BRETT: Prettily said.

KELLY: It's true.

BRETT: Pretty and true. What a combination. If I found
something both pretty and true...

KELLY: What would you do?

BRETT: Marry it. I thought.

KELLY: No counseling. You're right. We've overdosed
on the talking cure.

BRETT: Then what are we to each other?

(Beat)

KELLY: The world, to me, you are.

BRETT: Mm. Too much, never enough.

(Beat)

KELLY: Sometimes conversation, didn't you ever feel,
between us, was so easy, no one was speaking, the
words were responding to each other, we weren't using
them for anything, that it was language's day of rest,
too?

BRETT: Is it Sunday?

KELLY: It should be. It is a sunny day. We are at rest.

BRETT: The newspaper is enormous and almost devoid
of news.

KELLY: Sunday brunch working sessions. I loved those,
I loved feeling doubly productive, working through a

meal, on a day when working at all was taboo, fundamentalistically.

BRETT: Defiantly busy.

KELLY: And yet so often, mimosas. Let's be up here all day and think thoughts we love. If we could name our every antidote to suicide, would this go down as a red-letter day?

BRETT: Would it take a whole day, do you think?

KELLY: A few hours. Very rich hours.

BRETT: *Les Tres Riches Heures du Duc de Berry*. A private book of prayers.

KELLY: Against despair. The greatest sin.

(Beat)

BRETT: Remember years ago?

KELLY: I don't know if I can do this.

BRETT: I hadn't thought of this in forever. All I thought I wanted. Make love with you all night. Work on cars all day.

KELLY: When was this?

BRETT: Years ago. Can you imagine? Me so different.

KELLY: You haven't changed a whisker since we met. You never wanted to work on cars.

BRETT: Total shop rat. I loved it. It was such a corrective to my chatty self.

KELLY: Mechanics do not say sentences like that.

BRETT: I wasn't a real mechanic, I just liked to do it.

KELLY: This is some you you're imagining, I never knew this person.

BRETT: You don't remember. This kills me.

KELLY: When was this?

BRETT: When I got out of school? When I met you? The drifty year.

KELLY: I have a degree but I don't have an inkling?

BRETT: That period. You know this.

KELLY: I'd forgotten.

BRETT: I had this idea that this is a man's life. I was pretending I could be that kind of guy. That guy's guy.

KELLY: Did you ever tell me this?

BRETT: I thought I did. But you had such ideas about what I might become.

KELLY: So this is all my fault.

BRETT: What.

KELLY: You.

BRETT: No. You were a challenge. And that's another thing a man does, right, Rise to a Challenge. So I did that.

KELLY: I was so smart.

BRETT: Very.

KELLY: Very very smart.

BRETT: Though mostly I remember you as this wide open person.

KELLY: You do?

BRETT: I admired that. The honesty.

KELLY: Ha ha.

BRETT: Ha ha.

KELLY: Weren't we something.

BRETT: Well. You were. I was going to be.

KELLY: Me too.

BRETT: Ah well. Better luck next time.

KELLY: If only.

BRETT: No. True. *(Beat)* Why is it the greatest sin? Despair.

KELLY: Well. Once upon a time.

BRETT: Oh good.

KELLY: There was a belief. That all sins could be forgiven. By God. If the sinner makes a true repentance. And does her time in Purgatory. The one sin, unforgivable by God, is to lose all hope of His grace. That, by definition, is Hell.

BRETT: You should have married God.

KELLY: Well. Maybe that's why women taken in adultery, in the Middle Ages, if they survived, they'd be taken to a nunnery. To see each day a face that might possibly forgive them.

BRETT: And knowing all that did not stop them. And it didn't stop us.

KELLY: No.

BRETT: Why. Why.

KELLY: I think. There was a moment when I thought: this desire feels so strong. For something so foolhardy. In the face of all I feel for you. Placing everything that most matters to me at risk. That it must be very important to me. In a way that my mind cannot accept. It won't let me go. It must be real. Because I have had to learn, over years, to pay attention to the desires I cannot say I have. Those have always turned out to be the ones that were really mine. And not me trying to please my loved ones. So I disobeyed my conscience. And went deeper.

BRETT: Sounds like love.

KELLY: It does. But it was not love. It was not. I was raised to recognize this. It had a name. It was not love. It was...The Other Thing. As tempting as I was warned when I prepared for my First Communion and was without this kind of sin. But I stopped listening, at just the wrong age. And ever since then. I have lived, technically, in Hell.

BRETT: By that definition, so does everyone we know.

KELLY: Yes. And how about that: Hell doesn't feel bad at all, for a while. Just...a mite thin. So when that strong feeling comes over you, you feel...

BRETT: Good.

KELLY: You feel that you are right where you belong. You feel evil. But you've forgotten what to call it. And evil, like I said, is goodness that has forgotten its name. Despair is goodness that forgot how to get home.

(BRETT *stands.*)

KELLY: Where are you going?

BRETT: I'm making mimosas.

KELLY: For me too?

BRETT: I'm making two. If someone else happened to drink one, I wouldn't mind. Otherwise, it's seconds for me. Oof, all this coffee. I could piss off the roof, couldn't I? But that would betray everything I stand for. I might as well jump off as piss off.

KELLY: I couldn't either.

BRETT: Piss over the edge?

KELLY: It would betray everything I stand for.

(They stand at the edge. They look at each other. The lights fade.)

END OF PLAY

BROADWAY PLAY PUBLISHING INC

ADAPTATIONS OF THE CLASSICS

ALKI (PEER GYNT)

ANYTHING TO DECLARE?

THE BROTHERS KARAMAZOV

A CHRISTMAS CAROL

DEAD SOULS

DON JUAN

DON QUIXOTE DE LA JOLLA

THE FATHER

FIGARO/FIGARO

FRANK LANGELLA'S CYRANO

IL CAMPIELO

THE ILLUSION

JITTERBUGGING: SCENES OF SEX FROM A NEW SOCIETY
(LA RONDE)

MAN OF THE FLESH (DON JUAN)

THE MARRIAGE OF FIGARO

MCTEAGUE: A TALE OF SAN FRANCISCO

PLAYBOY OF THE WEST INDIES

THE PROMISE (THE DYBBUK)

THÉRÈSE RAQUIN

THREE SISTERS

BROADWAY PLAY PUBLISHING INC

PLAYWRIGHTS' COLLECTIONS

PLAYS BY NEAL BELL
MCTEAGUE: A TALE OF SAN FRANCISCO
RAGGED DICK
THÉRÈSE RAQUIN

PLAYS BY ALAN BOWNE
BEIRUT
FORTY-DEUCE
SHARON AND BILLY

PLAYS BY LONNIE CARTER
LEMUEL
GULLIVER
GULLIVER REDUX

PLAYS BY STEVE CARTER
DAME LORRAINE
HOUSE OF SHADOWS
MIRAGE
ONE LAST LOOK
TEA ON INAUGURATION DAY

PLAYS BY ANTHONY CLARVOE
LET'S PLAY TWO
THE LIVING
SHOW AND TELL

PLAYS BY DONALD FREED
ALFRED AND VICTORIA: A LIFE
CHILD OF LUCK
IS HE STILL DEAD?

PLAYS BY ALLAN HAVIS
HOSPITALITY
MINK SONATA
MOROCCO

PLAYS BY ALLAN HAVIS, VOLUME TWO
A DARING BRIDE
THE LADIES OF FISHER COVE
SAINTE SIMONE

PLAYS BY TONY KUSHNER
A BRIGHT ROOM CALLED DAY
THE ILLUSION
SLAVS!

PLAYS BY RICHARD NELSON
EARLY PLAYS VOLUME ONE
CONJURING AN EVENT
JUNGLE COUP
THE KILLING OF YABLONSKI
SCOOPING

PLAYS BY RICHARD NELSON
EARLY PLAYS VOLUME TWO
BAL
THE RETURN OF PINOCCHIO
THE VIENNA NOTES

PLAYS BY RICHARD NELSON
EARLY PLAYS VOLUME THREE
AN AMERICAN COMEDY
JITTERBUGGING: SCENES OF SEX IN A NEW SOCIETY
RIP VAN WINKLE, OR "THE WORKS"

PLAYS BY LOUIS PHILLIPS
BONE THE SPEED
CARWASH
CONRAD ON THE VINE
ETHIOPIA
THE MAN WHO ATE EINSTEIN'S BRAIN
PRECISION MACHINES

PLAYS BY AISHAH RAHMAN
THE MOJO AND THE SAYSO
ONLY IN AMERICA
UNFINISHED WOMEN CRY IN NO MAN'S LAND WHILE A BIRD DIES
IN A GILDED CAGE

PLAYS BY EDWIN SÁNCHEZ
CLEAN
FLOOR SHOW: DOÑA SOL AND HER TRAINED DOG
TRAFFICKING IN BROKEN HEARTS

PLAYS BY NAOMI WALLACE
IN THE HEART OF AMERICA
SLAUGHTER CITY
THE WAR BOYS

BROADWAY PLAY PUBLISHING INC

LONG ONE ACTS
(WRITTEN WITHOUT AN INTERMISSION)

BAL
(IN PLAYS BY RICHARD NELSON
EARLY PLAYS VOLUME TWO)

BEIRUT
(IN PLAYS BY ALAN BOWNE)

BETWEEN EAST AND WEST

BIG TIME

THE BEST OF STRANGERS
(IN FACING FORWARD)

FLOOR ABOVE THE ROOF

FLOOR SHOW: DOÑA SOL AND HER TRAINED DOG
(IN PLAYS BY EDWIN SÁNCHEZ)

HAITI (A DREAM)
(IN FACING FORWARD)

HARM'S WAY

THE HELIOTROPE BOUQUET BY SCOTT JOPLIN & LOUIS
CHAUVIN

HOLY DAYS

HOUSE OF SHADOWS
(IN PLAYS BY STEVE CARTER)

ICARUS

IS HE STILL DEAD
(IN PLAYS BY DONALD FREED)

JITTERBUGGING: SCENES OF SEX IN A NEW SOCIETY
(IN PLAYS BY RICHARD NELSON
EARLY PLAYS VOLUME THREE)

JUNGLE COUP
(IN PLAYS BY RICHARD NELSON
EARLY PLAYS VOLUME ONE

THE NIP AND THE BITE
(IN FACING FORWARD)

THE RETURN OF PINOCCHIO
(IN PLAYS BY RICHARD NELSON
EARLY PLAYS VOLUME TWO)

SEVENTY SCENES OF HALLOWEEN

SHARON AND BILLY
(IN PLAYS BY ALAN BOWNE)

TRAFFICKING IN BROKEN HEARTS
(IN PLAYS BY EDWIN SÁNCHEZ)

UNFINISHED WOMEN CRY IN A NO MAN'S LAND WHILE A
BIRD DIES IN A GILDED CAGE
(IN PLAYS BY AISHAH RAHMAN)

THE VIENNA NOTES
(IN PLAYS BY RICHARD NELSON
EARLY PLAYS VOLUME TWO)

THE WAR BOYS
(IN PLAYS BY NAOMI WALLACE)

BROADWAY PLAY PUBLISHING INC

ONE ACT COLLECTIONS

BIG TIME & AFTER SCHOOL SPECIAL

THE COLORED MUSEUM

ENSEMBLE STUDIO THEATER MARATHON `84

FACING FORWARD

GIANTS HAVE US IN THEIR BOOKS

ONE ACTS AND MONOLOGUES FOR WOMEN

ORCHARDS

ORGASMO ADULTO ESCAPES FROM THE ZOO

PLAYS BY LOUIS PHILLIPS

ROOTS IN WATER

SHORT PIECES FROM THE NEW DRAMATISTS

WHAT A MAN WEIGHS &
THE WORLD AT ABSOLUTE ZERO

BROADWAY PLAY PUBLISHING INC

TOP TEN BEST SELLING
FULL-LENGTH PLAYS AND
FULL-LENGTH PLAY COLLECTIONS

AVEN'U BOYS

THE BROTHERS KARAMAZOV

THE IMMIGRANT

ONE FLEA SPARE

ON THE VERGE

PLAYS BY TONY KUSHNER
(CONTAINING A BRIGHT ROOM CALLED DAY,
THE ILLUSION, & SLAVS!)

PLAYS BY AISHAH RAHMAN
(CONTAINING THE MOJO AND THE SAYSO,
UNFINISHED WOMEN...,
& ONLY IN AMERICA)

PRELUDE TO A KISS

TALES OF THE LOST FORMICANS

TO GILLIAN ON HER 37TH BIRTHDAY

BROADWAY PLAY PUBLISHING INC

PLAYS WITH MULTI-RACIAL CASTS

AVEN'U BOYS

FAR EAST

FLOOR ABOVE THE ROOF

FROM THE JOURNAL OF HAZARD MCCAULEY

GREEN CARD

GULLIVER

GULLIVER REDUX

IN THE HEART OF AMERICA

LEMUEL

SAINTE SIMONE

A SILENT THUNDER

SLAUGHTER CITY

STONEWALL JACKSON'S HOUSE

THE WHITE DEATH

BROADWAY PLAY PUBLISHING INC

PLAYS WITH ALL AFRICAN-AMERICAN CHARACTERS

THE COLORED MUSEUM

DAME LORRAINE

GENERATIONS OF THE DEAD IN THE ABYSS OF CONEY ISLAND MADNESS

THE HELIOTROPE BOUQUET BY SCOTT JOPLIN & LOUIS CHAUVIN

THE MOJO AND THE SAYSO

ONLY IN AMERICA

PECONG

PLAYBOY OF THE WEST INDIES

UNFINISHED WOMEN CRY IN NO MAN'S LAND WHILE A BIRD DIES IN A GILDED CAGE

BROADWAY PLAY PUBLISHING INC

PLAYS WITH MORE WOMEN THAN MEN

BESIDE HERSELF

A BRIGHT ROOM CALLED DAY

CHURCH OF THE HOLY GHOST

DAME LORRAINE

A DARING BRIDE

GOONA GOONA

THE LADIES OF FISHER COVE

MINK SONATA

ONLY IN AMERICA

ON THE VERGE

PECONG

PHANTASIE

RAIN. SOME FISH. NO ELEPHANTS.

SHOW AND TELL

STARSTRUCK

STONEWALL JACKSON'S HOUSE

UNFINISHED WOMEN WOMEN CRY IN NO MAN'S LAND
WHILE A BIRD DIES IN A GILDED CAGE

WHAT A MAN WEIGHS